**Nos encantan las ciencias
So Into Science!**

EXPLOREMOS
EL CLIMA
EXPLORING THE
WEATHER

Emmett Martin
Traducido por / Translated by Eida de la Vega

Gareth Stevens
PUBLISHING

Please visit our website, www.garethstevens.com. For a free color catalog of all our high-quality books, call toll free 1-800-542-2595 or fax 1-877-542-2596.

Library of Congress Cataloging-in-Publication Data

Names: Martin, Emmett, author.
Title: Exploring the weather = Exploremos el clima / Emmett Martin.
Description: New York : Gareth Stevens Publishing, [2019] | Series: So into science! = Nos encantan las ciencias | Includes index.
Identifiers: LCCN 2018013148| ISBN 9781538236307 (library bound)
Subjects: LCSH: Meteorology–Juvenile literature. | Weather–Juvenile literature.
Classification: LCC QC981.3 .M3668 2019 | DDC 551.5–dc23
LC record available at https://lccn.loc.gov/2018013148

Published in 2019 by
Gareth Stevens Publishing
111 East 14th Street, Suite 349
New York, NY 10003

Copyright © 2019 Gareth Stevens Publishing

Translator: Eida de la Vega
Editor, English: Therese Shea
Designer: Sarah Liddell

Photo credits: Cover, p. 1 Peter Gudella/Shutterstock.com; pp. 5, 13 (sun) AlinaMD/Shutterstock.com; pp. 7, 24 (thermometer) txking/Shutterstock.com; p. 9 Titood99/Shutterstock.com; p. 11 Alinute Silzeviciute/Shutterstock.com; p. 13 (park) Trong Nguyen/Shutterstock.com; p. 15 benemale/Shutterstock.com; p. 17 Romrodphoto/Shutterstock.com; p. 19 Anton Watman/Shutterstock.com; pp. 21, 24 (meteorologist) Joe Raedle/Staff/Getty Images News/Getty Images; p. 23 YukoF/Shutterstock.com.

All rights reserved. No part of this book may be reproduced in any form without permission in writing from the publisher, except by a reviewer.

Printed in the United States of America

CPSIA compliance information: Batch #CW19GS: For further information contact Gareth Stevens, New York, New York at 1-800-542-2595.

Contenido

¿Qué está pasando?. 4
Caliente y frío 6
Más palabras sobre el clima 12
El clima y la diversión. 22
Palabras que debes aprender 24
Índice 24

Contents

What's Happening?. 4
Hot and Cold 6
More Weather Words. 12
Weather Fun 22
Words to Know 24
Index. 24

El clima es lo que pasa en el aire a nuestro alrededor.

....

Weather is what's happening in the air around us.

5

Un termómetro nos dice la temperatura.

....

A thermometer tells us the temperature.

7

¡Hace calor!
Vamos a la playa.

....

It's hot!
We go to the beach.

9

¡Hace frío!
Patinamos sobre hielo.

....

It's cold!
We ice-skate.

11

¡Hace sol!
Vamos al parque.

....

It's sunny!
We go to the park.

13

¡Hace viento!
Volamos
una cometa.

....

It's windy!
We fly a kite.

15

¡Está lloviendo!
Saltamos en los charcos.

....

It's raining!
We jump in puddles.

17

¡Está nevando!
Hacemos ángeles
de nieve.
....

It's snowing!
We make snow angels.

19

Los meteorólogos
son científicos del clima.
Nos dicen cómo
va a estar el clima.

....

Meteorologists are
weather scientists.
They tell us what the
weather will be!

21

¡Yo siempre
me divierto
en cualquier tipo
de clima!

....

I have fun in all kinds
of weather!

23

Palabras que debes aprender
Words to Know

(la) meteoróloga
meteorologist

(el) termómetro
thermometer

Índice / Index

clima / weather 4, 20, 22

meteorólogo(a) / meteorologist 20

temperatura / temperature 6

termómetro / thermometer 6